Table of Contents

What is a Cave?

What are some things you think of when you read the word *cave*? Do you imagine bat wings fluttering, ears sleeping, tall ceilings, and narrow passages? All these can be found in caves, but there are many more things de the earth's underground spaces.

A cave is a hollow ace in the ground, g enough so that a rson can go inside it. me caves are as tiny closets, while others ve gigantic rooms as g as 14 football fields. me are mazes of nnels many miles long.

ny caves are filled with strange nations hanging from the ings and rising from the floors.

Most caves form in limestone, a kind of soft rock that dissolves in rainwater that contains acid. A cave can take millions of years to develop. During its history, it may be home to many different animals. Early humans lived in caves thousands of years ago. Today people visit caves—to study them and to admire their natural wonders.

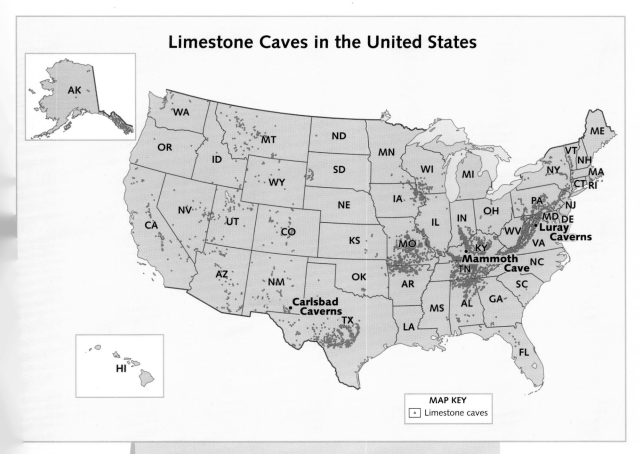

Limestone Caves in the United States

AK

WA
OR
ID
MT
ND
MN
WI
MI
ME
VT
NH
NY
MA
CT RI
PA
NJ
MD DE
Luray Caverns
WV
VA
OH
IN
IL
IA
SD
WY
NE
NV
CA
UT
CO
KS
MO
KY
Mammoth Cave
TN
NC
SC
GA
AZ
NM
OK
AR
AL
MS
Carlsbad Caverns
TX
LA
FL
HI

MAP KEY
▫ Limestone caves

What states would you visit to find limestone?

How Do Caves Happen?

Limestone caves don't all form in the same way, but most of them start with rainfall. Raindrops absorb carbon dioxide, a gas that animals breathe into the air. As rainwater seeps through the soil, it picks up a lot more carbon dioxide that is produced by decaying plants and animals. This mixture of water and carbon dioxide makes carbonic acid.

After seeping through the soil, the acid water reaches a layer of rock. The water works its way through the rock

How Limestone Caves Form

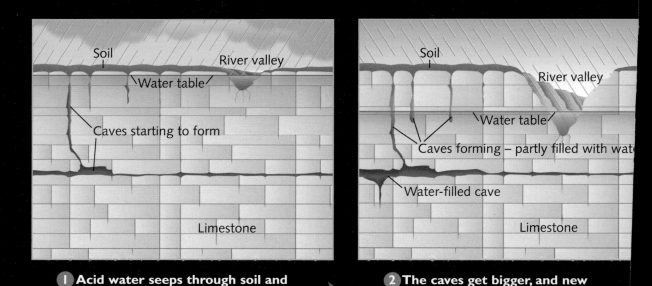

1 Acid water seeps through soil and down through cracks in limestone. The acid starts to dissolve the limestone.

2 The caves get bigger, and new ones form. A nearby river cuts deeper into the earth. Water starts to drain out of caves in upper layers of the limestone.

as well, trickling downward through cracks. At last the water reaches a level where all the cracks in the rock are already filled with water. The top of this level is called the **water table**.

A Cave Begins

If the rock is limestone, it starts to dissolve in the acid water below the water table. Slowly, over a few million years, the holes in the limestone get bigger, turning into caves and passageways.

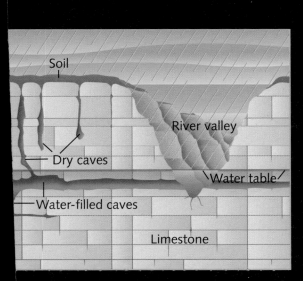

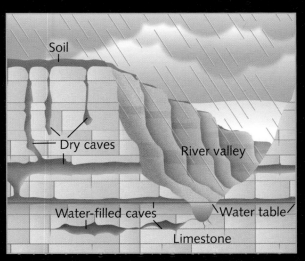

3 The river cuts even deeper. Caves in upper levels of the limestone are dry. Caves below the water table get bigger.

4 The river cuts down farther. The water drains out of more caves above the water table. New caves form below the water table, deep in the limestone. Can you find the cave entrances?

Limestone caves are also called "solution caves" because they are formed by an acid solution that dissolves the rock.

A cave can be filled with water for tens of thousands of years. Slowly rivers and streams flowing near the cave cut deeper and deeper **channels** in the ground. When these channels are deeper than the cave, the water from the cave drains into the channels through cracks in the limestone.

Most limestone caves are formed by carbonic acid. Others are formed by sulfuric acid. Bacteria that feed on oil deep in the earth give off a gas called hydrogen sulfide. As the gas rises through the earth, it mixes with water. Oxygen in the water combines with the gas to make sulfuric acid.

Like carbonic acid, sulfuric acid dissolves limestone, but it is stronger and forms caves faster. Recently scientists have discovered that bacteria living in some of these caves create even more sulfuric acid, which continues to eat away at the cave walls.

Sulfuric acid created Carlsbad Caverns in New Mexico.

A cave may have no entrance, or an entrance may appear long after the cave has formed. Sometimes an underground stream dissolves the wall of a cave, creating an opening. Sometimes a hillside **erodes** or a rock falls, uncovering a cave passage.

Cave Decorations

When water continues dripping into an empty cave, strange growths called **speleothems** may form on the floors and ceilings.

Stalactites, **stalagmites**, and columns are the most common speleothems. Others have wonderful names like gypsum flowers, draperies, cave pearls, popcorn, and totem poles. These formations are also known as cave decorations.

People need ropes and other special equipment to enter this cave in Alabama.

Cave Words

The word *speleothem* comes from two Greek words: *spelaion*, meaning "cave," and *thema*, meaning "deposit."

Speleology is the study of caves. *Speleologists* can be geologists, engineers, biologists, or archaeologists.

Spelunking is cave exploration. *Spelunkers* are also called cavers.

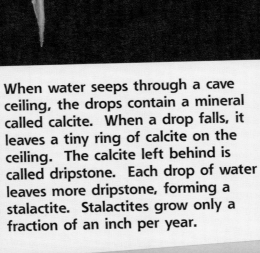

When water seeps through a cave ceiling, the drops contain a mineral called calcite. When a drop falls, it leaves a tiny ring of calcite on the ceiling. The calcite left behind is called dripstone. Each drop of water leaves more dripstone, forming a stalactite. Stalactites grow only a fraction of an inch per year.

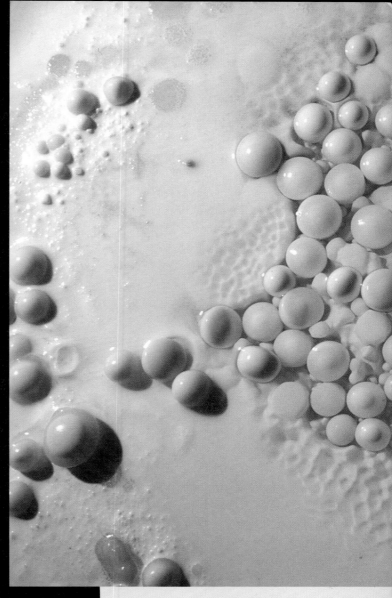

Water dripping from the cave ceiling also deposits tiny amounts of calcite on the floor. The calcite collects over thousands of years, forming stalagmites. A stalagmite usually forms under a stalactite. When a stalactite and a stalagmite meet, they form a column.

Cave pearls form in shallow cave pools. The calcite coats grains of sand.

What Lives in a Cave?

Many kinds of animals and plants live in caves, and some are just as strange as the caves' decorations. Different **organisms** live in different parts of the cave.

Black bears often spend the winter in caves.

The Light Zone

The light zone is the area near the entrance of a cave. There, one may find footprints of animals that spend some time in the cave but don't stay there permanently. Deer, raccoons, skunks, snakes, mice, and bears go into caves seeking shelter. Owls may nest in the rocky walls of a cave near the opening. Mosses, ferns, and mushrooms may grow near the cave entrance.

The Twilight Zone

Deeper inside the cave is the twilight zone. Here, there is only dim light, not enough to see very well. People exploring this zone need a flashlight to move without running into a wall or a pile of rocks.

Some owls nest in the twilight zone. Slimy salamanders lay their eggs in puddles here. Daddy longlegs scurry across the dark cave floor on spindly legs. **Lichens** and mosses grow on the damp rocks.

Some animals that live in the twilight zone leave the cave to look for food.

The Dark Zone

This zone is so far inside the cave that no outside light can reach it. The animals that live here don't need light. Most of them spend their whole lives in caves.

This cave spider is blind and colorless.

Creatures of the dark zone don't need light in order to live. Some have eyes that can't see, while others have no eyes at all. These animals survive by using their senses of smell and touch. Many are colorless because they don't need **pigment** to protect them from the sun. Animals of the dark zone include spiders, flatworms, salamanders, beetles, and millipedes—a creepy, crawly bunch!

Food is limited in the dark zone, since no green plants can grow here. Insects and other small creatures eat bacteria and **fungi** that grow on bat droppings, called **guano**. They also feed on dead animals and plant material carried into the cave by water or by visitors. Larger animals eat the smaller ones.

Bats live in the dark zone during the day but fly out at night in search of insects.

Underground River Dwellers

Underground rivers flow through many caves. These rivers may flow for miles in complete darkness, sometimes connecting with other rivers and streams. Animals such as cave fish, salamanders, and tiny buglike **crustaceans** often live in these dark underground waters.

This blind crayfish lives in Echo River in Mammoth Cave, Kentucky.

Like other animals of the dark zone, cave river animals are **adapted** to life without light. Most of them are colorless and small.

Cave river animals have adapted to survive on only a few sources of food. These animals compete for bacteria, one-celled animals, fungi, and flatworms. When floods wash bark, seeds, and leaves in from the ground above, the cave river creatures have a feast!

A stream flows through a passage in Nutt Cave in West Virginia.

Some cave salamanders lose their eyesight as they grow up, but many are born blind.

Blind cave salamanders lay their eggs in the river water, where they hatch. Some cave salamanders can see at birth, but because they never need their eyes, their eyelids grow together. Their bodies lose the color they had at birth and become pale. Then the salamanders crawl out of the river to live on the cave floor.

Several species of cave fish live in underground rivers. The blindfish of Mammoth Cave is one of the largest animals found in cave rivers, but it is only about four inches long. It has sightless eyes, or no eyes at all. Instead, it uses sensitive whiskers to feel its way around the cave and detect the movement of other animals.

Blindfish eat whatever they can find, including their own babies. When a baby blindfish senses the movement of larger blindfish nearby, it becomes very still to avoid being eaten.

Blindfish are colorless and almost transparent.

Humans and Caves

Very long ago, early humans lived in caves. Caves protected people from wild animals and bad weather. Today, **archaeologists** study caves to learn more about the people who used them.

In Russell Cave in Alabama, archaeologists have found weapons, tools, pottery, and other things left behind by Native Americans long ago. Different groups used the cave as a winter home for almost 10,000 years.

People sometimes decorated the walls of caves with paintings and drawings. This painting is found in Mammoth Cave, Kentucky. What do you think it shows?

Geologists study caves to learn how old they are, how they formed, and how they are still changing. Geologists also learn many other things from caves. By studying cave fill—material that has washed into a cave from outside— they can learn how the land near the cave developed and even what the climate was like in the past.

Some cave geologists study water pollution. In caves they can follow water underground and see where it goes. They learn how water polluted in one place affects people's drinking water in another place.

These bacteria, seen under a powerful microscope, live on the rock walls of sulfuric-acid caves.

Microbiologists go into caves to study organisms that live where humans or other animals cannot. Some scientists think these organisms show that there could be life on other planets.

Some people visit caves as tourists, to admire their natural wonders. Spelunkers enjoy exploring caves for excitement, adventure, mystery, and physical challenge.

If you visit a cave, look but don't touch. Caves that took thousands of years to form can be ruined in minutes. Broken stalactites and stalagmites can't be repaired. You should follow the saying, "Take only photos, leave only footprints."

Cave Safety

Caving can be very dangerous. People who explore caves must follow safety rules.

- Never explore a cave alone or without an adult.
- Always carry several sources of light.
- Carry backpacks with food, water, and first aid kits.
- Wear warm, sturdy clothing and boots and have the right equipment.

Cavers use equipment like that of mountain climbers—chest harnesses, helmets, strong ropes, sturdy shoes, and special tools for climbing.

Famous U.S. Caves

There are thousands of limestone caves in the United States. Many of them are protected by the National Park Service. Three famous cave systems that people can visit are Mammoth Cave, Carlsbad Caverns, and Luray Caverns.

Mammoth Cave

Native Americans discovered this cave system thousands of years ago, in what is now Kentucky. Archaeologists have found remains of their sandals and torches. These first explorers collected a mineral called gypsum, which they may have used in medicines.

This is one of many huge rooms in Mammoth Cave.

Tourists have visited Mammoth Cave since 1839. Stephen Bishop, a 17-year-old slave, was its first and most famous guide. He discovered 10 miles of major tunnels. An early guidebook describes the cave's wonders—steep cliffs, an underground river, huge stone pillars, and rock formations with names like the Giant's Coffin and the Devil's Armchair.

Mammoth Cave is the world's longest cave system. So far, nearly 350 miles of passageways and rooms have been mapped.

Carlsbad Caverns

In the late 1890s, a young cowboy named Jim White was riding his horse in southern New Mexico. Suddenly he saw smoke rising from the earth. As he rode closer, he realized that what looked like smoke was actually millions of bats, flying out of a deep hole in the ground. The hole was an opening into Carlsbad **Caverns**.

Jim White was not the first person to find the entrance to the caverns, but he was the first to explore them. For the next 20 years, he tried to interest other people in the wonders he had found. He told everyone he could about the "ghost-like totem poles," "frozen cascades of glittering flowstone," and other natural wonders. Today, thanks to White's efforts, Carlsbad Caverns National Park protects the cavern and more than 100 other caves near it.

Carlsbad Caverns is one of the world's largest cave systems. Its rooms are full of stalactites, stalagmites, and other decorations. Explorers and guides have given the rooms colorful names such as "Bat Cave," "Queen's Chamber," and "King's Palace."

The "Big Room" in Carlsbad Caverns is the size of 14 football fields!

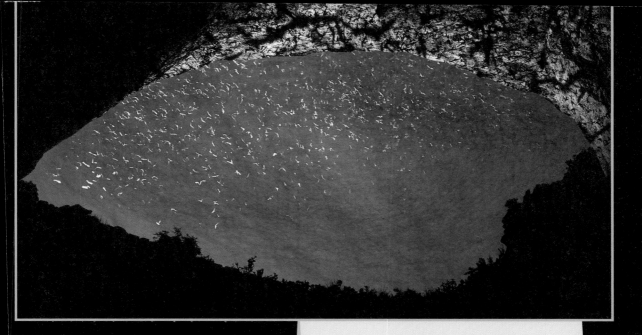

Free-tailed bats leave Carlsbad Caverns at dusk.

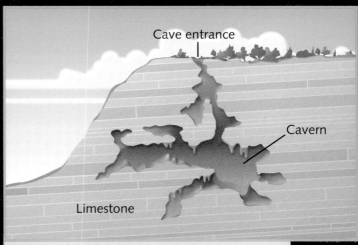

Cave entrance

Cavern

Limestone

On the surface, the only clue to a cavern like Carlsbad is the entrance. How would you explore this cavern? What do you think you would find?

27

Luray Caverns

Thirteen-year-old Quint Campbell, his uncle Andrew, and three other men were looking for caves in the Shenandoah Valley of Virginia in 1878. Suddenly, a wind rushed out of a hole in the ground and blew out a candle one of the men was holding.

Quint and the men dug away loose rocks and dangled a rope into the hole. They carefully slid down into what proved to be one of the biggest caves in the eastern United States. It was filled with stalactites and stalagmites, sparkling in the candlelight. This underground wonderland came to be called Luray Caverns, named for the town near the cave.

The colors in Luray Caverns are produced by minerals in the water that seeps into the cave.

Protecting Caves

Caves are still being discovered. Many limestone caves lie beneath the Tongass National Forest in Alaska. Every summer, members of the Tongass Cave Project explore and map these caves. They have found bones of humans and animals that lived in the caves long ago. The members of the Tongass Cave Project are working to protect these caves so we can continue to learn from them.

Caves are natural treasures. They contain some of the strangest and most beautiful sights on Earth. They also contain a wealth of information about Earth, about plants and animals, and about humans. If we protect them, caves will amaze and teach us for many years to come.

Scientists study cave animals to learn how they have adapted to survive in these unusual places.

Glossary

adapt: change in order to survive in a particular kind of place

archaeologist: a scientist who studies past human life through fossils, tools, and other remains of ancient peoples

cave: a hollow space in the earth big enough for a person to go inside

cavern: a cave, especially a large one

channel: a hollowed-out place in the earth where water flows, such as the bed of a stream or river

crustacean: an animal belonging to a large group, called Crustacea, that includes shrimp, lobsters, and crabs. Most crustaceans live in water.

erode: wear away rocks and soil, usually by wind, water, or ice

fungus: a flowerless plantlike organism that usually lives on dead or decaying plant or animal material. More than one fungus are called *fungi*.

geologist: a scientist who studies the history of Earth, mainly by studying rocks

guano: partly decayed bat or bird droppings

lichen: a plantlike organism that is partly a fungus and that grows on a surface such as a rock

microbiologist: a scientist who studies living things that are too small to see without a microscope

organism: a living thing

pigment: a natural coloring material in animals and plants

speleothem: a cave deposit or formation

stalactite: a formation that grows down from the ceiling of a cave

stalagmite: a formation that grows up from the floor of a cave

water table: the top of the level in the earth where all the cracks in the rock are filled with water

Index

To explore another cave, visit this Website:
www.colossalcave.com